A LAND OF CHARM AND GRANDEUR

江山如此多娇

当代世界出版社

THE CONTEMPORARY WORLD PUBLISHING HOUSE

A LAND OF CHARM AND GRANDEUR

江山如此多娇

当代世界出版社

THE CONTEMPORARY WORLD PUBLISHING HOUSE

《江山如此多娇》编辑委员会 Editorial Board

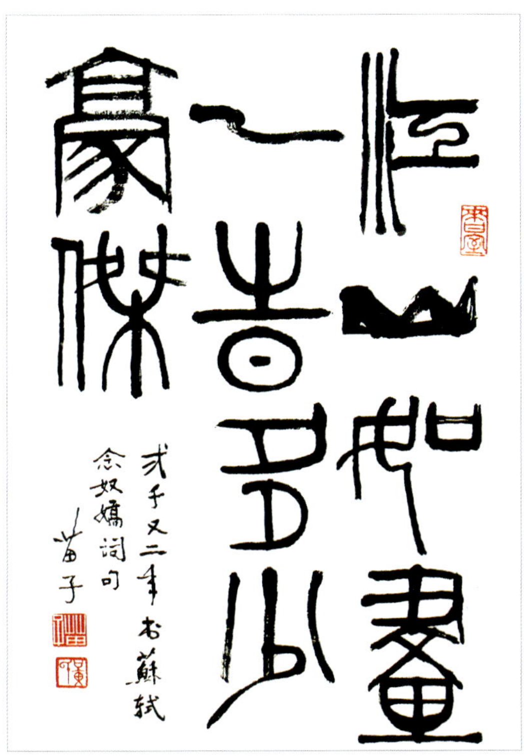

序

常有一些国外的朋友要我介绍中国最美的风景名胜，由于文化的差异，一时又找不到精美的画册推荐给他们，所以总是留下遗憾。这就好像绘画，胸中丘壑，难于表达，总不满意。

有关“江山”的摄影成籍是一件吃力不讨好的事情。其实百姓有百姓的“江山”，帝王有帝王的“江山”，我有我心中的江山，你也有你心中的江山，如何协调呢，是很费脑筋的。不过朋友要我为画册作序，总要搜肠刮肚说上一些不中听的话。

前些年，一些文化散文类的书倒是提了不少好地方，据说影响了很多人，还有人按图索骥，专程跑到这些原产地去旅游、体验，于是又一批现代美文问世，精美的照片更是层出不穷，出版界自然也忙得不亦乐乎。当然也有人起来表示反对，说文化散文追求的是文化效应，其中不乏主观臆断，有的还引来不少官司。我想，文人毕竟是文人，还是绕不开自己那些关于“江山”、关于“历史”的情结。照片则不同了，尽管山川风物已今非昔比，但是透过光学机械眼记录的影像还是真实可信的。这也是我要说的几句话。既然是摄影，就要尽可能地逼近自然，逼近原生态，尽管摄影也有主观感受，但摄影也必须有感而发。拍照的人在大自然面前被感动，拍出的照片也会感动别人，当然还有技术问题。反正我这个老头子是做不来的。

摄影人，千万不要因为散文中的“白发苏州”就一定要在镜头中去寻找苏州的老态，历史是长了点，并非就是一个“老”字。苏州的灵动的生态若是放到大的历史观中还是很年轻，甚至是超前的，摄影创作如不能领会这一点是不行的。这真有些教训人的味道了，我的本意还是在讲一个“真”字。时下年轻人的通病是对艺术的规律掌握不多，文化底蕴不够厚。其实到了一定程度上，物艺是相通的，艺术家不但要业有所专，更需要有广博而深厚的文化底蕴，这样才能取得一点成绩。

中国大地，幅员辽阔，山川秀美，风物也各异，中华文化更是博大精深。整理工作是很繁琐的，但凡是工作就要有个态度。我对于文物和世界遗产，心敬仰之，却对有些整理工作不以为然。一些所谓的改造与修缮，同样延续着“白发即老”的思维，还美其名曰“修旧如旧”，这种对于时间的态度是不对的。20世纪60年代初我写《八大山人传》一直到最近的重写，“流光容易把人抛”，单这一篇《传》，已经抛去了三十多年的时光了。“锦屏人忒看得韶光贱”，《牡丹亭》这句曲子，反复读之，别是一番滋味！而现代人又似乎太讲究效率了，关键是能否禁得住时间的检验，希望这本画册能弥补一些遗憾。画册形成之前，编者似乎并没有一个现成的思维约束，而是以宏观呈现为主，尽可能还原原本的、真正的“多娇的江山”，这是一种贡献。所谓“看山还是山、看水还是水”，这些图片，都是熟悉的，要让看出其中不熟悉的地方来，才见功力。以上算是我对这本画册的一点褒奖与希望吧。

苗子

PREFACE

Many of my overseas friends often ask me to depict the beautiful landscapes and scenic spots in China. I always regret to have failed them, owing partly to the cultural differences and partly to the dearth of a fine and handy picture album to present to them. It's just like that frustrated kind of feeling of a painter when he has the whole picture with all the details in mind but only find it hard to spell it out on the canvas.

To compile a landscape photo album is a tough but thankless job given the truth that everybody sees the same landscape in a different way. The same mountains and rivers may look completely different in the eyes of a king than in the eyes of a vagabond. It is indeed a brain-consuming task to make it pleasing to all. However, obliged to a friend for a preface of the album, I cannot but rack my brains for a few words, which may not sound so pleasant to some people.

A couple of years ago, quite a few nice places were well mentioned in some cultural essay books. Those books became all the rage and it is said that many readers even made their way to the original places by following the clues in the books, trying to locate and testify the beauty of the described spots. As a result, the following years saw a surge of more exquisite writings with all the splendid pictures coming thick and fast, to the great delight of publishers. Naturally some people argued against it, blaming that these books were merely after cultural effects. Some of the arguments were more out of conjectures and even brought in a number of lawsuits. That is what men of letters are meant for, perhaps. They are bound to be obsessed with their own complex about "landscapes" and "history". But photos are different. No matter how things change in the passage of time, images captured by optical lenses remain true and reliable. This is one of the points I'm trying to make. Photography by its name means to present nature as true as it is, although photographers do have feelings of their own and must reflect their emotions in their works. When a picture taker is affected by the scene in front of the shutter, his photos will affect others. Of course skills also count, and that will never become a piece of cake for my senile self.

A lensman should never try to look deliberately for decrepitude from Suzhou city simply because he read about the "gray-haired Suzhou" in those essays. Suzhou does have a long history, to be true, but it does not simply mean it is "decrepit". In a greater perspective of history, Suzhou, with its keen and vivacious state of life, is fairly a young city, and even an avant-garde. One cannot be a good artist if he doesn't see this point. It may sound like lecturing, but what I mean is to emphasize the word "truth". A failing that is common to young people nowadays is that they know little about the rules of art and do not have a good grounding in the learning of culture. Art and nature are in fact interlinked especially when it comes to a certain stage. An artist must have the expertise, of course, but more importantly, he must also be a learned person with profound knowledge of culture, if he is to achieve anything.

China has a vast territory with beautiful landscapes and multifarious sceneries, and has an extensive and profound culture in particular. We can imagine the sifting and sorting out of pictures must be a tedious work. But all work requires effort and needs a right attitude. When I have a reverent affection to cultural relics and world heritages, I would not commend the way they are preserved in some places. Some rebuilding and renovation projects are still being carried out in the belief that "gray hair denotes old age", and are claimed to be "reproducing the antique look". That is not the right attitude towards time.

Talking about time, it is amazing to perceive how it flies. 30-odd years have flown away between my first writing of the Biography of Zhu Da (also know as Pa-ta Shan-jen) in the early 1960s and the recent rewriting! Just as the line goes in Peony Pavilion: "The spring time is drifting away too swiftly for the lady behind the screen". Chewing over the words from the old drama, you will find a special savour in it. But it seems that people in our modern times are giving too much value to efficiency, putting durability, which is much more important, to the neglect. Hopefully this collection can be of some remedy for the regret. It's a pleasant thing to see that the compilers have not bound their minds with any clichéd thinking and have tried their best to present us a real and true macroscopic "land of charm and splendour". This is quite a meritorious deed. As is said in dhyana meditation, when you have come to the apex state, you'll see "mountains still as mountains and rivers still as river". The pictures collected in this album are mostly of familiar scenes, but a high caliber cameraman can always exhibit a unique image of an ordinary view.

With these words, I convey my commendations and expectations to this praiseworthy work.

Huang Miaozi

目　录 CONTENT

东 EAST 6

西 WEST 78

南 SOUTH 168

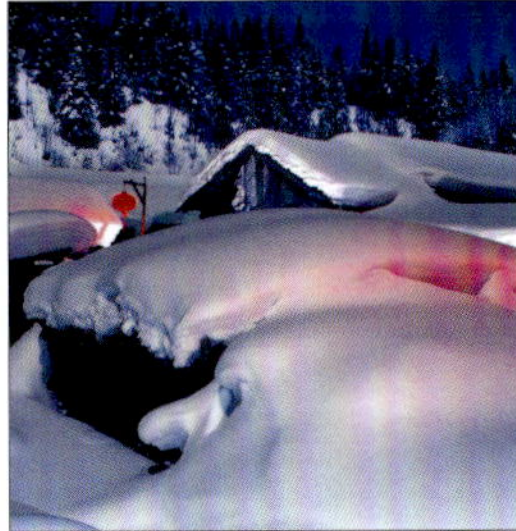

北 NORTH 234

中 MIDDLE 300

五嶽獨尊
昂頭天外

日出东方

东方，不是一个简单的地理概念。中国历史上的三国时期，一代枭雄曹操征战乌桓，在这里曾面对太阳和大海写下了气吞山河的豪迈诗句："东临碣石，以观沧海"。"日月之行，若出其中"...... 此后的一千八百多个岁月，中华民族始终没有停止过对统一富强的艰难寻觅，直至20世纪中下叶，中华人民共和国宣告成立后，一批具有现代化工业文明的国际大都市和经济高新技术开发区在这一带崛起。这里山川毓秀，人文荟萃，五岳独尊，秦淮一脉，十里洋场，西湖水月，东海渔舟，武夷秀色，大江东去，淘尽千古......

The East — Where the Sun Rises

The East is not simply a geographic term. During the period of the Three Kingdoms in the Chinese history, the fierce and ambitious hero Cao Cao came to the eastern coast on his way to conquer his enemies. This is where he composed the gallant poem with these famous lines:

"East of Jieshi mountain, I gaze at the blue sea."

"The path of the sun and moon, seems to come from within."

In the following 1,800 odd years, the Chinese nation has never remitted its effort in probing the way to unification and prosperity. Since the middle of the 20th century after the founding of the People's Republic, numbers of metropolitan cities, economic development zones and hi-tech industrial parks sprang into being along the eastern coast, apart from the ever bustling city of Shanghai. This part of the country is not only endowed with abundant wealth of culture and a galaxy of talents, but also boasts famous natural sceneries that include the Mount Tai -- the most revered among the "Five Sacred Mountains" in China, the verdant Mount Wuyi, the Qinhuai River that gives life to Najing city, the graceful West Lake reflecting the full moon, and the ceaseless flow of the Yangtze River that runs into the vast and blue East China Sea.

上海东方明珠电视塔
The Oriental Pearl TV Tower, Shanghai

上海人民广场
People's Square, Shanghai

雅戈尔

上海外滩夜景 Night view of the Bund, Shanghai

上海中共一大会址 Site of the First Congress of the Communist Party of China, Shanghai

上海淀山湖风光 Dianshanhu Lake, Shanghai

上海方塔 Fangta Pagoda, Shanghai

上海豫园 Yuyuan Garden, Shanghai

上海陆家嘴金融贸易区夜景 吕玉民／摄影
Night View of the Lujiazui Financial and Trade Zone Photographer: Lyu Yumin

江苏南京中山陵 卞志武／摄影
Mausoleum of Dr. Sun Yat-sen, Nanjing, Jiangsu Province. Photographer: Bian Zhiwu

江苏苏州狮子林 卞志武／摄影
Lions' Forest, Suzhou, Jiangsu Province. Photographer: Bian Zhiwu

江苏苏州网师园 卞志武／摄影
Wangshiyuan Garden, Suzhou, Jiangsu Province. Photographer: Bian Zhiwu

江苏苏州拙政园 卞志武／摄影
Zhuozhenyuan Garden, Suzhou, Jiangsu Province. Photographer: Bian Zhiwu

江苏苏州退思园 卞志武／摄影
Tuisiyuan Garden, Suzhou, Jiangsu Province. Photographer: Bian Zhiwu

江苏苏州留园 卞志武／摄影
Liuyuan Garden, Suzhou, Jiangsu Province. Photographer: Bian Zhiwu

江苏扬州瘦西湖风光　马恒福／摄影　View of Shouxihu Lake, Yangzhou, Jiangsu Province. Photographer: Ma Hengfu

江苏扬州瘦西湖月观 王虹军／摄影
Hall of Moon, Shouxihu Lake, Yangzhou, Jiangsu Province. Photographer: Wang Hongjun

江苏扬州盐商古宅　马恒福／摄影
Ancient Mansion of salt merchant, Yangzhou, Jiangsu Province. Photographer: Ma Hengfu

江苏扬州高邮湖风光 马恒福／摄影
Scenery of Gaoyouhu Lake, Yangzhou, Jiangsu Province. Photographer: Ma hengfu

江苏昆山周庄 王俊峰／摄影

Zhouzhuang, Kunshan, JIangsu Province. Photographer: Wang Junfeng

江苏盐城大丰麋鹿国家级自然保护区 杨国美／摄影
Dafeng Deer National Sanctuary, Yancheng, Jiangsu Province. Photographer: Yang Guomei

左上：江苏徐州茅村汉画像石墓 郑云峰／摄影

Above left: Stone tomb with paintings of Han Dynasty at Maocun village, Xuzhou, Jiangsu Province. Photographer: Zheng Yunfeng

左中：江苏徐州狮子山西汉兵马俑军阵 徐瑞吉／摄影

Middle left: Terra-cotta of West Han Dynasty at Mt.Lion, Xuzhou, Jiangsu Province. Photographer: Xu Ruiji

左下：江苏徐州白集汉墓墓室 邵 艳／摄影

Below left: Coffin Chamber of the Baiji Tomb, Xuzhou, Jiangsu Province. Photographer: Shao Yan

江苏徐州龟山汉墓墓室 郑云峰／摄影

Coffin Chamber of the Guishan Tomb of Han Dynasty, Xuzhou, Jiangsu Province. Photographer: Zheng Yunfeng

浙江杭州六和塔 刘德安／摄影
Liuhe Pagoda in Hangzhou, Zhejiang Province.
Photographer: Liu De'an

浙江钱塘江大潮 杨佐桓／摄影
Springtide of Qiangtangjiang River, Zhejiang Province. Photographer: Yang Zuoheng

浙江杭州西湖风光 卞志武／摄影

Scenery of West Lake in Hangzhou, Zhejiang Province. Photographer: Bian Zhiwu

浙江东海渔舟 萧 越/摄影
Fishing boats in the East China Sea, Zhejiang Province. Photographer: Xiao Yue

浙江丽水仙都 吴品禾／摄影
Scenery of the "Fairy Land" at Lishui County, Zhejiang Province. Photographer: Wu Pinghe

浙江淳安千岛湖风光 彭小枫／摄影
Scenery of Qiandao Lake in Chun'an, Zhejiang Province. Photographer: Peng Xiaofeng

浙江雁荡山风光 张侯权／摄影
Scenery of Mt. Yandang, Zhejiang Province. Photographer: Zhang Houquan

中国新千年第一缕曙光洒落在风光旖旎的浙江省温岭市石塘镇 曾凡祥／摄影
The first sunray of the new millennium upon Shitang town, Wenling City, Zhejiang Province. Photographer: Zeng Fanxiang

浙江武义宣莲　梅安才／摄影
Lotus in Wuyi, Zhejiang Province. Photographer: Mei Ancai

浙江普陀山寺院　洪晓明／摄影
Temples in Mt. Putuo, Zhejiang Province. Photographer: Hong Xiaoming

福建武夷山风光　卞志武／摄影
Scenery of Mt. Wuyi, Fujian Province. Photographer: Bian Zhiwu

福建泉州洛阳桥 蒋长云／拍摄
Luoyang Bridge in Quanzhou, Fujian Province. Photographer: Jiang Changyun

福建福州金山寺 陈良森／摄影
Jinshan Temple in Fuzhou, Fujian Province. Photographer: Cheng Liangsen

福建厦门南普陀寺 谢明俊／摄影
Temple of Nanputuo in Xiamen, Fujian Province. Photographer: Xie Mingjun

福建泉州双塔——西塔　郑启东／摄影
West Tower of the Twin Tower in Quanzhou, Fujian Province. Photographer: Zheng Qidong

福建泉州双塔——东塔　郑启东／摄影
East Tower of the Twin Tower in Quanzhou, Fujian Province. Photographer: Zheng Qidong

福建泉州老君岩 郑启东/摄影
Lao Zi Rock in Quanzhou, Fujian Province. Photographer: Zheng Qidong

福建厦门集美　朱庆福／摄影
Jimei Village in Xiamen, Fujian Province. Photographer: Zhu Qingfu

福建厦门鼓浪屿风光　郑启东／摄影
Scenery of Gulangyu Islet in Xiamen, Fujian Province. Photographer: Zheng Qidong

江西三清山风光 李建惠／摄影

Scenery of Mt. Sanqing, Jiangxi Province Photographer: Li Jianhui

江西庐山三叠泉　邹树汉／摄影
Scenery of Sandie Spring in Mt. Lushan, Jiangxi Province. Photographer: Zhuo Shuhan

江西庐山含鄱口　邹树汉／摄影
Scenery of Hanbokou Pass in Mt. Lushan, Jiangxi Province. Photographer: Zhuo Shuhan

江西鄱阳湖鞋岛 刘兴庞／摄影
Scenery of the Shoe Island in Poyanghu Lake. Jiangxi Province. Photographer: Liu Xinglu

江西安远三百山风光 赖国柱／摄影
Scenery of Mt. Sanbai in An'yuan, Jiangxi Province. Photographer: Lai Guozhu

江西龙虎山晨曦　池晓虹／摄影
A glimmer of dawn at Dragon and Tiger Mountain, Jiangxi Province. Photographer: Chi Xiaohong

江西湖口石钟山 刘兴鹿／摄影

Mt. Shizhong in Hukou, Jiangxi Province. Photographer: Liu Xinglu

江西白鹿洞书院　饶金星／摄影
Bailudong Academy, Jiangxi Province. Photographer: Rao Jinxing

江西景德镇陶瓷历史博览区 郑筱卿／摄影
Exhibition Park of Porcelain History in Jingdezhen, Jiangxi Province. Photographer: Zheng Xiaoqing

江西景德镇"吉祥如意"釉中彩中餐具 郑筱卿／摄影
"Good luck" tableware of color glazed porcelain, Jingdezhen, Jiangxi Province. Photographer: Zheng Xiaoqing

江西新余仙女湖风光 周瑞生／摄影
Scenery of Fairy Lake in Xinyu, Jiangxi Province. Photographer: Zhou Ruisheng

江西吉安茨坪 池晓虹／摄影
Scenery of Ciping village in Ji'an, Jiangxi Province. Photographer: Chi Xiaohong

江西井冈山风光　曾凡祥／摄影
Scenery of Mt. Jinggang, Jiangxi Province. Photographer: Zeng Fanxiang

安徽黄山日出 张永富／摄影
Sunrise at Mt. Huangshan, Anhui Province. Photographer: Zhang Yongfu

安徽黄山双剪峰 郑启东／摄影
Peak Scissors in Mt. Huangshan, Anhui Province.
Photographer: Zheng Qidong

安徽黄山云海 张永富／摄影
Sea of clouds over Mt. Huangshan, Anhui Province.
Photographer: Zhang Yongfu

安徽黄山风光 陆开蒂／摄影
Scenery of Mt. Huangshan, Anhui Province. Photographer: Lu Kaidi

安徽屯溪老街 郑启东／摄影
Old street in Tunxi, Anhui Province. Photographer: Zheng Qidong

安徽巢湖帆影 张恣宽／摄影
Scenery of Chaohu Lake, Anhui Province. Photographer: Zhang Cikuan

安徽歙县石潭风光　刘少宁／摄影
Scenery of Shitan Village, She County, Anhui Province. Photographer: Liu Shaoning

安徽九华山天台正顶 张慈宽／摄影
The top of Mt.Jiuhua, Anhui Province. Photographer: Zhang Cikuan

安徽歙县棠樾牌坊群 郑启东／摄影
The Memorial Archway in She county, Anhui Province. Photographer: Zheng Qidong

安徽黟县宏村古民居 郑启东／摄影
Traditional Dwelling houses in Hongcun Village, Anhui Province. Photographer: Zheng Qidong

安徽黟县西递古民居 张慈宽／摄影
Traditional Dwelling houses in Xidi Village, Anhui Province. Photographer: Zhang Cikuan

山东泰山日出 郑启东／摄影
Sunrise on Mt.Tai, Shandong Province. Photographer: Zheng Qidong

山东泰山五岳独尊
"The Most Revered among the Five Sacred Mountains", Mt. Tai, Shandong Province.

山东曲阜孔庙
Confucian Temple, Qufu, Shandong Province

山东曲阜孔林 杨佐桓／摄影
Confucian Woodland, Qufu, Shandong Province. Photographer: Yang Zuoheng

山东曲阜孔庙大成殿　杨佐桓／摄影

Great Perfeciton Hall, Confucian Temple, Qufu, Shandong Province.

Photographer: Yang Zuoheng

山东济南大明湖风光
Scenery of Daminghu Lake, Jinan, Shandong Province

山东济南趵突泉
The Baotu Spring, Jinan, Shandong Province

山东青岛栈桥
The Landing Stage, Qingdao, Shandong Province

山东青岛崂山风光
Scenery of Mt. Laoshan in Qingdao, Shandong Province

山东荣成成山头风光
Scenery of Chenshantou Rock, Rongcheng, Shandong Province

山东曲阜少昊陵
Shaohao's Tomb, Qufu, Shangdong Province

山东蓬莱阁
Penglai Pavilion, Shandong Province

山东长岛宝塔礁
The Treasure Pagoda Reef at Long Island, Shandong Province

神奇西部

西部——最令华夏儿女骄傲的地方。公元1298年，意大利旅行家马可·波罗在狱中口述他的东方见闻，第一次将中国介绍给西方世界。一部《马可·波罗游记》使他名垂青史，据专家考证，当年马可·波罗就是从新疆西部的帕米尔高原沿古丝绸之路进入中国的。从世界屋脊到戈壁绿洲；从丝绸之路到唐蕃古道；香格里拉，版纳风情；三峡云雨，川江号子；九寨红枫，都江古堰；三江源头，大漠孤烟；八井地热，天山宝藏；和田美玉，滚滚石油；归去来兮，中华西部如醉如梦……

The West —a Land of Mystical Charm

The western region is a pride of the descendants of Cathay. In 1298, China was introduced for the first time in history to the Occidental world through The Travels of Marco Polo, a record of the narrations from an Italian traveler Marco Polo about his experience in the Orient. According to textual researches, Marco Polo came into China from the Pamirs in the west of today's Xingjiang Uygur Autonomous Region along the ancient Silk Road. In this wonderland in the west of the country, you will gasp in admiration at the enthralling scenes from the Qinghai-Tibet Plateau known as the Roof of the World, to the Gobi desert and its oasis, from the Silk Road and Tangfan Ancient Road to the world admired Shangri-La, and again to the exotic kingdoms of flora and fauna in Xishuangbanna. You will also be intoxicated by the hazy look of the Three Gorges with boat trackers chanting work songs on the Chuanjiang River, the legendary Jiuzhai Valley covered with red autumnal leaves, and the wilderness of the boundless desert. Still amazing are the magnificent ancient irrigation project Dujiangyan, the welling springs that give source to three big rivers, the misty geo-thermal fields in Yangbajing of Tibet, as well as hills and plains that hold in store rich reserves of precious minerals and other resources.

擎天三柱 高晓春／摄影

Three Pillars into the Heaven, Tibet. Photographer: Gao Xiaochun

西藏大昭寺金顶法轮 王志文／摄影
The Wheel of Law in Jokhang Temple, Tibet. Photographer: Wang Zhiwen

西藏布达拉宫 岱天荣／摄影
The Potala Palace, Tibet. Photographer: Dai Tianrong

西藏古格王国遗址 扎 堆／摄影
Ruins of Ancient Guge Kingdom, Tibet. Photographer: Zha Dui

西藏纳木错 魏胜利／摄影
The Namtso Lake, Tibet. Photographer: Wei Shengli

西藏空喀山韵 王安民／摄影
Mt. Kongka, Tibet. Photographer: Wang

西藏雅鲁藏布江大峡谷 岱天荣／摄影

The Grand Canyon of Brahmaputra River, Tibet. Photographer: Dai Tianrong

西藏沱沱河 李 映／摄影
Tuotuo River, Tibet. Photographer: Li Ying

云南梅里雪山风光 迟玉洁／摄影
Scenery of Snow-Capped Mt. Meili, Yunnan Province. Photographer: Chi Yujie

云南梅里雪山日出　刘建明／摄影
Sunrise on Mt. Meili, Yunnan Province. Photographer: Liu Jianming

云南西双版纳橄榄坝风光 刘建明／摄影
Scenery of Olive Dam in Xishuang-banna, Yunnan Province. Photographer: Liu Jianming

云南西双版纳曼飞龙白塔 刘建明／摄影
White Pagoda in Xishuang-banna, Yunnan Province. Photographer: Liu Jianming

云南西双版纳野象谷 刘建明／摄影
Wild Elephant Valley in Xishuang-banna, Yunnan Province. Photographer: Liu Jianming

云南丽江古城与玉龙雪山 刘建明／摄影
Old City of Lijiang and Yulong Snow Mountain, Yunnan Province. Photographer: Liu Jianming

云南丽江古城 王文平／摄影
Old City of Lijiang, Yunnan Province. Photographer: Wang Wenping

云南元阳梯田 陈鸣文／摄影

Terraced fields in Yuanyang, Yunnan Province. Photographer: Chen Mingwen

云南元阳梯田 宋举浦／摄影

Terraced fields in Yuanyang, Yunnan Province. Photographer: Song Jupu

云南石林 卞志武／摄影

Stone Forest, Yunnan Province. Photographer: Bian Zhiwu

云南大理洱海 刘建明／摄影

The Erhai Lake in Dali, Yunnan Province. Photographer: Liu Jiangming

云南大理三塔 刘建明／摄影
Dali Santa (Triple towers), Yunnan Province.
Photographer: Liu Jiangming

云南滕冲叠水河瀑布 刘建明／摄影
The Waterfall on Dieshuihe River in Tengchong, Yunnan Province. Photographer: Liu Jiangming

云南腾冲火山群 刘建明／摄影
Volcanos in Tengchong, Yunnan Province. Photographer: Liu Jiangming

云南香格里拉松赞林寺之晨 刘建明／摄影
Dawnbreak at the Songzanling Temple, Shangli-ra, Yunnan Province. Photographer: Liu Jiangming

云南滇池风光 卞志武／摄影
Scenery of Dianchi Lake, Yunnan Province. Photographer: Bian Zhiwu

云南罗平油菜花 宋举浦／摄影
Rape flowers in Louping, Yunnan Province. Photographer: Song Jupu

云南石鼓长江第一湾 贾建新/摄影
The first bend of the Yangtzi River, Shigu, Yunnan Province. Photographer: Jia Jianxin

云南泸沽湖风光 刘建明／摄影
Scenery of Luguhu Lake, Yunnan Province. Photographer: Liu Jiangming

云南罗平九龙瀑布 刘建明／摄影
Nine-dragon Waterfall in Luoping, Yunnan Province. Photographer: Liu Jiangming

贵州贵阳黔灵山鸟瞰 贺培铨／摄影
A Bird view of Mt. Qianling in Guiyang, Guizhou Province. Photographer: He Peiquan

贵州黄果树瀑布 贺培铨／摄影
The Huangguoshu Waterfall, Guizhou Province. Photographer: He Peiquan

贵州遵义会议会址 梅印生／摄影
The site of Zunyi Meeting, Guizhou Province. Photographer: Mei Yinsheng

贵州贵阳文昌阁 贺培铨／摄影
The Wenchang Pavilion in Guiyang, Guizhou Province. Photographer: He Peiquan

贵州贵阳阿哈湖风光　陈　慧／摄影
Scenery of Ahahu Lake in Guiyang, Guizhou Province. Photographer: Cheng Hui

贵州梵净山风光　高　平／摄影
Scenery of Mt. Fanjing, Guizhou Province.
Photographer: Gao Ping

贵州赤水十丈洞瀑布 贺培铨／摄影

The Shizhangdong Waterfall in Chishui, Guizhou Province. Photographer: He Peiquan

贵州赤水竹海 贺培铨／摄影

The bamboo forest in Chishui, Guizhou Province. Photographer: He Peiquan

贵州贵阳甲秀楼 卞志武／摄影
Jiaxiu Pavilion in Guiyang, Guizhou Province. Photographer: Bian Zhiwu

贵州贵阳红枫湖风光 贺培铨／摄影
Scenery of Red Maple Lake in Guiyang, Guizhou Province. Photographer: He Peiquan

四川峨眉山风光 王达军／摄影
Scenery of Mt. Ermei, Sichuan Province.
Photographer: Wang Dajun

四川都江堰 崔　伟/摄影
The Dujiangyan Dam, Sichuan Province. Photographer: Cui Wei

四川乐山大佛 王达军／摄影
The Buddha statue in Mt. Leshan, Sichuan Province. Photographer: Wang Dajun

四川若尔盖九曲黄河第一湾 王瑞林／摄影
The first bend of Yellow River in Nou'ergai, Sichuan Province. Photographer: Wang Ruilin

四川小金县四姑娘山
李同喜／摄影
Mt. Siguniang in Xiaojing County, Sichuan Province.
Photographer: Li Tongxi

四川央迈勇雪山
高晓春／摄影
Snow mountain in Yangmaiyong, Sichuan Province. Photographer: Gao Xiaochun

四川成都杜甫草堂　卞志武／摄影
Du Fu Cottage in Chengdu, Sichuan Province. Photographer: Bian Zhiwu

四川广汉三星堆遗址 王达军／摄影
Sanxingdui Relic in Guanghan, Sichuan Province. Photographer: Wang Dajun

四川红原麦洼寺转山会　王瑞林／摄影
Buddha Bathing Festival in Hongyuan, Sichuan Province. Photographer: Wang Ruilin

四川丹巴藏居 刘双发／摄影

Tibetan Residential House in Danba, Sichuan Province. Photographer: Liu Shuangfa

四川青城山 崔 伟 / 摄影 Mt.Qingcheng, Sichuan Province. Photographer: Cui Wei

四川成都望江楼 王达军／摄影
River-view Pavilion in Chengdu, Sichuan Province. Photographer: Wang Dajun

四川广元皇泽寺 张 雷／摄影
The Huangze Temple in Guangyuan, Sichuan Province.
Photographer: Zhang Lei

左上：四川九寨沟风光 卞志武／摄影
Above left: Scenery of Jiuzhaigou Valley, Sichuan Province. Photographer: Bian Zhiwu
左下：四川黄龙风光 王达军／摄影
Below left: Scenery of Huanglong, Sichuan Province. Photographer: Wang Dajun

四川九寨沟镜海红枫 杨佐桓/摄影
Red maple in Jinghai lake, Jiuzhaigou Valley, Sichuan Province. Photographer: Yang Zuoheng

四川九寨沟诺日朗瀑布 杨佐桓／摄影 Nuorilang waterfall in Jiuzhaigou Valley, Sichuan Province. Photographer: Yang Zuoheng

重庆渝中半岛 罗大万／摄影
The Yuzhong Peninsular, Chongqing. Photographer: Luo Dawan

重庆合川涞滩瓮城 罗大万／摄影
The enceinte of Laitan city gate in Hechuan, Chongqing. Photographer: Luo Dawan

重庆瞿塘峡夔门 罗大万／摄影
Qutangxia Gorge, Chongqing. Photographer: Luo Dawan

重庆江津四面山望乡台瀑布 罗大万／摄影
The Wangxiangtai waterfall in Jiangjin, Chongqing.
Photographer: Luo Dawan

重庆大足石刻 崔　伟／摄影
Dazu stone carving, Chongqing. Photographer: Cui Wei

重庆江津中山古镇　罗大万／摄影
Zhongshan ancient town in Jiangjin, Chongqing. Photographer: Luo Dawan

青海青海湖鸟岛 卞志武／摄影
Bird Island in Qinghai Lake, Qinghai Province. Photographer: Bian Zhiwu

青海青海湖鸬鹚岛 梁建军／摄影
Cormorant Island, Qinghai Lake, Qinghai Province. Photographer: Liang Jianjun

青海玉树文成公主庙 梁建军／摄影
Temple of Princess Wencheng in Yushu, Qinghai Province. Photographer: Liang Jianjun

青海果洛州甘德县隆恩塔 梁建军／摄影
The Long'en Stupa in Gande County, Qinghai Province. Photographer: Liang Jianjun

青海隆宝滩 李　伟／摄影
The Longbaotan Natural Reserve, Qinghai Province. Photographer: Li Wei

新疆天山天池 卞志武／摄影
Heavenly Lake, Mt. Tianshan, Xinjiang. Photographer: Bian Zhiwu

新疆天山冬韵 李学亮／摄影
Mt. Tianshan in winter, Xinjiang. Photographer: Li Xueliang

新疆塔克拉玛干沙漠 岱天荣／摄影
Takla Makan Desert, Xinjiang. Photographer: Dai Tianrong

新疆帕米尔高原地貌　岱天荣／摄影
Pamirs Plateau, Xinjiang, Photographer: Dai Tianrong

新疆天山一号冰川
晏　先／摄影
No.1 glacier on Mt. Tianshan, Xinjiang.
Photographer: Yan Xian

新疆吐鲁番苏公塔 晏 先／摄影
Sugong Minaret, Turpan, Xinjiang. Photographer: Yan Xian

新疆喀什阿巴克霍加陵墓 晏 先/摄影
The Apak Hoja Tomb, Karshgar, Xinjiang. Photographer: Yan Xian

新疆南疆风光 王安民／摄影
Scenery in Southern Xinjiang. Photographer: Wang Anmin

新疆公格尔九别峰 李学亮／摄影

Peak of Kongur Tobe, Xingjiang, Photorapher: Li Xueliang

新疆火焰山 李学亮／摄影 The Flaming Mountain, Xinjiang. Photographer: Li Xueliang

新疆吐乌大高速公路和风力发电厂 晏　先／摄影
The Turpan-Urumuqi Highway and Windmill, Xinjiang. Photographer: Yan Xian

新疆喀纳斯卧龙湾 郑启东／摄影
The Wolong Bay of Kanas, Xinjiang. Photographer: Zheng Qidong

新疆喀纳斯月亮湾 王长江／摄影
The Moon bay of Kanas, Xinjiang. Photographer: Wang Changjiang

新疆布尔津五彩滩 侯小勤／摄影
Colorful Shoal in Burjin, Xinjiang. Photographer: Hou Xiaoqing

新疆魔鬼城 郑启东／摄影
Ghost Castle, Xinjiang. Photographer: Zheng Qidong

新疆喀纳斯冬韵 晏 先/摄影
Kanas in Winter, Xinjiang. Photographer: Yan Xian

新疆白哈巴风光 王长江／摄影
Scenery of White Haba Village, Xinjiang. Photographer: Wang Changjiang

台湾合欢山云海 陈斌华／摄影
Sea of Clouds over Mt. Hehuan, Taiwan. Photographer: Cheng Binhua

台湾阿里山姊妹潭 叶 芳／摄影
Sister Lake in Mt. Ali, Taiwan. Photographer: Ye Fang

台湾花莲峡谷　魏胜利／摄影
The Hualian Canyon, Taiwan. Photographer: Wei Shengli

台湾台南郑成功受降塑像 陈斌华／摄影

The Status of "Hero Zheng Chengong recovering Taiwan", Taiwan. Photographer: Cheng Binhua

左：台湾屏东鹅銮鼻灯塔 叶 芳／摄影
Left: Light House in Pingtung City, Taiwan. Photographer: Ye Fang

右：台湾南部海上的小琉球 陈斌华／摄影
Right: An Islet to the South of Taiwan, Taiwan. Photographer: Cheng Binhua

台湾台北野柳女王头 叶 芳／摄影
Rock of Queen's Head, Yeliu, Taipei, Taiwan. Photographer: Ye Fang

台湾台东三仙台 叶 芳／摄影
Sanxiantai in Taitung, Taiwan. Photographer: Ye Fang

台湾高雄港 陈斌华／摄影
Port of Kaohsiung, Taiwan. Photographer: Ye Fang

台湾台东初鹿牧场 叶 芳／摄影
Chulu Ranch in Taitung, Taiwan. Photographer: Ye Fang

香港铜锣湾时代广场 陈树坚／摄影
Time Square at Causeway Bay, Hong Kong. Photographer: Chen Shujian

香港维多利亚港风光 郑启东／摄影

Scenery of Victoria Bay, Hong Kong. Photographer: Zheng Qidong

香港仔深湾海鲜舫和游艇会 徐志光／摄影
Yacht Club in the Deep Bay, Hong Kong. Photographer: Xu Zhiguang

香港铜锣湾商业区 欧阳耀文／摄影
Shopping Center in Causeway Bay, Hong Kong. Photographer: Euyang Yaowen

圣诞装饰下的香港 徐志光／摄影
Hong Kong at Christmas Day, Hong Kong. Photographer: Xu Zhiguang

香港尖沙咀钟楼 朱国樑／摄影
Bell Tower in Tsim Sha Tsui, Kowloon. Hong Kong. Photographer: Zhu Guoliang

现代化的中国银行大厦和长江中心，与古朴典雅的立法会大楼和旧中国银行大厦互相辉映。陈树坚／摄影

The Bank of China Tower and Cheung Kong Center loom over the Legislative Council Building and the old Bank of China Building. Photographer: Chen Shujian

上：香港荃湾三栋屋

Above: Cottage in Tsuen Wan, Hong Kong

下：香港米埔沼泽区中的反嘴鹬 朱国樑／摄影

Below: A Pied Avocet in Mai Po wet land, Hong Kong. Photographer: Zhu Guoliang

香港国际机场 徐志光／摄影
Hong Kong International Airport. Photographer: Xu Zhiguang

香港中环 Central Plaza, Hong Kong

香港大屿山大佛 郑启东／摄影
Big Buddha on Lantau Island, Hong Kong. Photographer: Zheng Qidong

香港青马大桥 郑启东／摄影
Tsing Ma Bridge, Hong Kong. Photographer: Zheng Qidong

澳门国际烟花汇演
The International Fireworks Display Contest, Macao.

澳门妈阁庙
A-Ma Temple, Macao.

澳门东望洋灯塔
Guia Fort & Lighthouse, Macao.

澳门大三巴牌坊
Ruins of St. Paul's, Macao.

澳门西湾湖广场
Sai Van Lake Square, Macao.

澳门格兰披治大赛车
Grand Phix , Macao.

澳门国际马拉松比赛
International Marathon, Macao.

澳门离岛住宅式博物馆
Taipa House Museum, Macao.

澳门议事亭前地
Largo do Senado, Macao.

澳门卢廉若花园
Lou Lim Ieoc Garden, Macao.

海南海棠湾鸟瞰 黄克峰／摄影
A bird view over Haitang Bay, Hainan Province. Photographer: Huang Kefeng

海南文昌椰林 卞志武／摄影
Coconut Grove at Wenchang, Hainan Province. Photographer: Bian Zhiwu

海南万泉河　杨佐桓／摄影
Wanquan River, Hainan Province. Photographer: Yang Zuohuan

海南万泉河漂流　蒙钟德／摄影
Drifting along the Wanquan River, Hainan Province. Photographer: Meng Zhongde

海南天涯海角 卞志武／摄影
The End of the Earth, Hainan Province. Photographer: Bian Zhiwu

海南三亚大东海 卞志武／摄影
Dadonghai Tourist Resort at Sanya, Hainan Province. Photographer: Bian Zhiwu

海南博鳌国际会议中心 杨佐桓／摄影
A corner of the Boao International Conference Center, Hainan Province. Photographer: Yang Zuohuai

海南南山寺 黄克峰／摄影
Nanshan Buddhist Temple, Hainan Province. Photographer: Huang Kefeng

海南儋州东坡书院的苏东坡铜像 柯人俊／摄影
The bronze statue of famous poet Su Dongpo at the Dongpo Academy of Classic Learning, Hainan Province. Photographer: Ke Renjun

广东肇庆七星岩 卞志武／摄影
Seven-star Rocks at Zhaoqing, Guangdong Province. Photographer: Bian Zhiwu

广东深圳金融中心区　韦洪兴／摄影
Financial District at Shenzhen, Guangdong Province. Photographer: Wei Hongxing

右上：广东深圳世界之窗 郑启东／摄影

Above right: The Window of the World at Shenzhen, Guangdong Province. Photographer: Zheng Qidong

右下：广东深圳中华民俗文化村“泼水节” 刘伯良／摄影

Below right: Water Splashing Festival at the Chinese Folk Culture Village of Shenzhen, Guangdong Province. Photographer: Liu Boliang

广东佛山清晖园
Qinghui Garden at Foshan, Guangdong Province.

广东深圳沙河高尔夫球场 刘伯良／摄影
Shahe Golf Course at Shenzhen, Guangdong Province. Photographer: Liu Boliang

广西阳朔风光 卞志武/摄影
Sceneries in Yangshuo, Guangxi. Photographer: Bian Zhiwu

上：广西桂林象鼻山 林文洪／摄影
Above: Elephant Trunk Hill at Guilin, Guangxi. Photographer: Lin Wenhong
下：广西桂林芦笛岩溶洞 莫文兴／摄影
Below: Reed Flute Cave at Guilin, Guangxi. Photographer: Wu Wenxing

广西桂林漓江风光 李自岐／摄影
Lijiang River, Guilin, Guangxi. Photographer: Li Ziqi

广西龙胜龙脊梯田 李文升／摄影
Dragon's Back Rice Terraces at Longsheng of Guangxi. Photographer: LI Wensheng

广西资源八角寨风光 秦卫东／摄影
Bajiaozhai at Ziyuan of Guangxi. Photographer: Qin Wendong

广西三江侗族风雨桥 滕　荣／摄影
Wind and Rain Bridge of Dong nationality at Sanjiang of Guangxi Photographer: Teng Rong

广西南丹白裤瑶族风情 周军伊／摄影
Customs of Baikuyao ethnic group at Nandan of Guangxi Photographer: Zhou Junyi

广西柳州夜景 梁家积／摄影
Night view of Liuzhou City, Guangxi. Photographer: Liang Jiaji

广西宁明花山壁画 区 阳／摄影
Cliff Paintings on Floral Hill at Ningming, Guangxi. Photographer: Qu Yang

广西漓江风光 王国强／摄影
Lijiang River, Guangxi. Photographer: Wang Guoqiang

广西乐业天坑　张小宁／摄影
Karst Tiankeng at Leye of Guangxi Photographer: Zhang Xiaoning

广西防城港虾场 莫尚义／摄影
Shrimp farm at Fangcheng Harbor of Guangxi Photographer: Mo Shangyi

广西三娘湾一瞥 杨小武／摄影
A glance over Sanniang Bay, Guangxi. Photographer: Yang Xiaowu

广西德天瀑布 卞志武／摄影
Detian Waterfall, Guangxi. Photographer: Bian Zhiwu

湖南衡山雾凇 刘柏林／摄影
Frost Fog at Mt. Hengshan, Hunan Province. Photographer: Liu Bolin

湖南衡山风光 刘春林／摄影
Scenery of Mt. Hengshan, Hunan Province. Photographer: Liu Chunlin

湖南凤凰城风光 冯根锁／摄影
The Town of Phoenix, Hunan Province. Photographer: Feng Gensuo

湖南凤凰古城风光 胡勇明／摄影
The Town of Phoenix, Hunan Province. Photographer: Hu Yongming

湖南长沙爱晚亭 龚智强／摄影
Aiwan pavilion at Changsha City, Hunan Province. Photographer: Gong Zhiqiang

湖南长沙世界之窗 郑启东／摄影
The Window of the World at Changsha, Hunan Province. Photographer: Zheng Qidong

湖南张家界风光 卞志武／摄影
Zhangjiajie Natural Forest Park, Hunan Province. Photographer: Bian Zhiwu

湖南张家界天女撒花 陈启辉／摄影
Zhangjiajie Natural Forest Park, Hunan Province. Photographer: Chen Qihui

湖南张家界风光 徐昌俊/摄影
Zhangjiajie Natural Forest Park, Hunan Province. Photographer: Xu Changjun

湖南岳阳楼 Yueyang Pavilion, Hunan Province.

N

富饶北疆

北疆，千里沃野，高踞雄鸡之冠。有河西故道、莫高石窟、贺兰岩画、沙漠胡杨；有西出阳关、长河落日、呼伦碧草、肥美牛羊；有茫茫林海、朔风吹雪、长白天池、镜泊湖光；有扎龙丹鹤、大连新港、吉林雾凇、北大粮仓。"我看江山多妩媚，料江山看我应如是……"

The North—Fertile Frontiers

Occupying the high top of the rooster-shaped territory of the country with a vast expand of fertile soil, Northern China is renowned not only for the famous historic sites like the Hexi Ancient Road, the Mogao Grotto Complex, the Yangguan Pass on the Great Wall and the rock paintings in the Helan Mountains, but also for the picturesque scenes like the endless desert decorated by diversiform leaved poplars, the majestic volcanic lakes on top of the Changbai Mountain and on the Mudan River, immense forests covered in white snow, and red-crowned cranes enjoying life in their well protected colony in Zhalong wetland. More to be found are thriving herds of sheep and cattle grazing on luxuriant prairies, billowing grain fields bearing bumper harvests in the former "great northern wilderness" as well as giant vessels coming in and out the busy port of Dalian…

内蒙古鄂温克旗冰雪"那达慕" 白海琦／摄影
Nadam Festival in the Erwenki Banner, Inner Mongolia. Photographer: Bai Haiqi

内蒙古陈巴尔虎左旗风光 白海琦／摄影
Scenery of the Chenba Erhu Left Banner, Inner Mongolia. Photographer: Bai Haiqi

内蒙古岩画 杨 孝／摄影
Ancient Cliff Painting, Inner Mongolia. Photographer: Yang Xiao

内蒙古鄂尔多斯成吉思汗陵 杨 孝／摄影
Tomb of Genghis Khan in Ordos, Inner Mongolia. Photographer: Yang Xiao

内蒙古呼和浩特五塔寺 杨 孝／摄影
The Temple of Five Pagodas in Hohhot, Inner Mongolia.
Photographer: Yang Xiao

内蒙古陈巴尔虎旗呼和诺尔风光 白海琦／摄影
Scenery of the Huhenuo'er, Chenba Erhu Banner, Inner Mongolia. Photographer: Bai Haiqi

内蒙古鄂温克旗雪景 白海琦／摄影
Snow scenery of the Erwenki Banner, Inner Mongolia. Photographer: Bai Haiqi

内蒙古阿拉善盟胡扬 杨 孝／摄影
Diversiform Leaved poplar trees in Alxa League, Inner Mongolia. Photographer: Yang Xiao

内蒙古呼伦贝尔草原——莫尔格勒河 杨 孝／摄影
Moergele River, the Hulunbuir prairie, Inner Mongolia. Photographer: Yang Xiao

上：草原壮士　刘长城／摄影
Above: Wrestlers. Photographer: Liu Changcheng
下：内蒙古贺兰山广宗寺　杨　孝／摄影
Below: Guangzong Temple in Mt. Helan, Inner Mongolia. Photographer: Yang Xiao

内蒙古呼伦贝尔草原　朱　民／摄影
The Hulunbuir Prairie, Inner Mongolia. Photographer: Zhu Min

内蒙古额济纳旗风光 张 翎／摄影
Scenery of the Ejina banner, Inner Mongolia. Photographer: Zhang Ling

内蒙古额济纳旗黑城遗址 杨 孝／摄影

Site of the Ancient Black City, the Ejina Banner, Inner Mongolia. Photographer: Yang Xiao

甘肃嘉峪关关城 Great Wall at Jiayuguan Pass, Gansu Province.

甘肃嘉峪关长城第一墩
The First Fortress of the Great Wall at Jiayuguan Pass, Gansu Province.

甘肃敦煌月牙泉
Crescent Moon Lake at Dunhuang, Gansu Province.

甘肃敦煌鸣沙山 卞志武／摄影
Mingsha Sand Dunes at Dunhuang, Gansu Province. Photographer: Bian Zhiwu

甘肃麦积山石窟 张茂松／摄影
Grottos on Mt. Maiji, Gansu Province. Photographer: Zhang Maosong

甘肃敦煌莫高窟 卞志武／摄影
Dunhuang Mogao Grottoes, Gansu. Photographer: Bian Zhiwu

甘肃嘉峪关魏晋墓
Ancient Tomb of Wei and Jin Dynesty, Jiayuguan Pass, Gansu Province.

甘肃嘉峪关魏晋墓壁画
Grave Fresco of Wei and Jin Dynesty, Jiayuguan Pass, Gansu Province.

甘肃玉门关 Yumen Pass, Gansu Province.

甘肃雅丹地貌
Yardang Landform, Gansu Province.

甘肃永靖恐龙足印化石群
Fossils of Dinosaur Footprints at Yongjing, Gansu Province.

甘肃甘南草原
Prairie in Southern Gansu, Gansu Province.

甘肃兰州市夜景
Night view of Lanzhou City, Gansu Province.

宁夏石嘴山古长城遗址 乔 华／摄影
Ruins of the Great Wall at Mt. Shizuishan, Ningxia. Photographer: Qiao Hua

宁夏永宁风光 徐毅仁／摄影
Scenery of Yongning , Ningxia. Photographer: Xu Yiren

宁夏六盘山云海 刘宪忱／摄影
Cloud Sea at Mt. Liupanshan , Ningxia. Photographer: Liu Xianchen

宁夏贺兰山岩画　刘立祥／摄影
Cliff Painting at Mt. Helan, Ningxia. Photographer: Liu Lixiang

宁夏青铜峡一百零八塔 徐胜凯／摄影
108 Buddhist Stupas at Qingtong Gorge, Ningxia. Photographer: Xu Shengkai

宁夏西夏王陵 刘立祥／摄影

Mausoleum of the King of Xixia Kingdom, Ningxia. Photographer: Liu Lixiang

宁夏中卫沙坡头 刘宪忱／摄影
Sand Slopes in Zhongwei County, Ningxia. Photographer: Liu Xianchen

宁夏西吉丹霞地貌 徐胜凯／摄影

The Danxia Landform in Xiji County, Ningxia. Photographer: Xu shengkai

宁夏水洞沟遗址 徐胜凯／摄影
Shuidonggou Relic, Ningxia. Photographer: Xu Shengkai

宁夏银川海宝塔 刘宪忱／摄影
Haibao Pagoda at Yinchuan, Ningxia. Photographer: Liu Xianchen

宁夏银川承天寺塔 张万集／摄影
Pagoda in Chengtian Temple, Yinchuan , Ningxia. Photographer: Zheng Wanji

宁夏平罗沙湖风光　惠　冰／摄影
Scenery of the Sand Lake, Pingluo County, Ningxia. Photographer: Hui Bing

黑龙江镜泊湖冬景　王　立／摄影
Winter of the Jingpo Lake, Heilongjiang Province. Photographer: Wang Li

黑龙江镜泊湖　郑启东／摄影
Jingpo Lake, Heilongjiang Province. Photographer: Zheng Qidong

黑龙江齐齐哈尔扎龙风光 徐大可／摄影
Scenery of Zhalong, Qiqihar, Heilongjiang Province. Photographer: Xu Dake

黑龙江齐齐哈尔扎龙霞光 穆祥滨／摄影
Zhalong at the dawn, Qiqihar, Heilongjiang Province. Photographer: Mu xiangbin

黑龙江大海林雪乡 李 野／摄影

Dahailin village after snowfall, Heilongjiang Province. Photographer: Li Ye

黑龙江绥化庆安良田 白海琦／摄影
Fertile soil at Qing an, Suihua, Heilongjiang Province. Photographer: Bai Haiqi

吉林长白山 肖 鸣／摄影

Mt. Changbaishan Natural Reserve, Jilin Province. Photographer: Xiao Ming

吉林长白山天池 郎 琦／摄影
Tianchi Lake at Mt. Changbaishan Natural Reserve, Jilin Province. Photographer: Liang Qi

吉林长白山 魏敏学／摄影
Mt. Changbaishan Natural Reserve, Jilin Province. Photographer: Wei Xuemin

吉林长白山风光 李建惠／摄影
Scenery of Mt. Changbaishan, Jilin Province. Photographer: Li Jianhui

吉林长白山溶岩峰 肖 鸣／摄影
Mt. Changbaishan Natural Reserve, Jilin Province. Photographer: Xiao Ming

吉林长白山雾凇　肖　鸣／摄影

Frost Fog at Mt. Changbaishan Natural Reserve, Jilin Province. Photographer: Xiao Ming

吉林靖宇松花江风光 肖 鸣／摄影
Songhuajiang River, Jilin Province.
Photographer: Xiao Ming

吉林鸭绿江秋色 肖 鸣／摄影
Yalujiang River in autumn, Jilin Province. Photographer: Xiao Ming

吉林高山苔原 肖 鸣／摄影
Mountain Tundra, Jilin Province. Photographer: Xiao Ming

吉林向海丹顶鹤　赵　俊／摄影
Red-crowned cranes at Xianghai Natural Park, Jilin Province. Photographer: Zhao Jun

辽宁鞍山千山金刚峰云海　翁光天／摄影
Cloud sea at Jingang Peak, Mt. Qianshan, Anshan, Liaoning Province. Photographer: Wonng Guangtian

辽宁本溪五女山 贺 兵／摄影
Mountain of Five Ladies, Benxi, Liaoning Province. Photographer: He Bin

左上：辽宁鞍山雪景 牛玉亮／摄影

Above left: Snow scene of Anshan, Liaoning Province. Photographer: Niu Yuliang

左下：辽宁本溪风光 王 宏／摄影

Below left: Scenery of Benxi City, Liaoning Province. Photographer: Wang Hong

辽宁大连夜色 Night view of Dalian City, Liaoning Province.

辽宁盘锦仙鹤 Cranes at Panjin, Liaoning Province.

辽宁盘锦红海滩
Red Beach of Panjin, Liaoning Province.

辽宁锦州港
Jinzhou Port, Liaoning Province.

M

雄强中原

中原，漫长三千五百年，一直是中国政治文化经济的中心。传说大禹治水把天下分为九州，每州一鼎，象征着中华先祖权覆九州的一统大志。古云：得中原者得天下。而今，中原大地依旧是生机勃勃气象万千。南有衔江黄鹤，荆楚胜迹，三峡平湖，神龙森林，武当奇峰；中踞嵩山古寺，少林英雄，黄帝故里，上明清河，千里平原；西拥秦川百里，出土兵俑，平遥古城，黄河玉壶，嵯峨华山；北呈长城要塞，山海一关，避暑山庄，白洋水泊，燕赵城郭。而特别之处还在于首都北京，这里演绎着中华民族最动人的篇章。俱往矣，江山如此多娇……

The Midland —Full of Masculine Vigour

Over 3500 years, the central plains have remained China's political, economic and cultural center. In the legend, the ancient flood fighting hero Dayu casted nine bronze vessels, representing sovereignty over the nine states in ancient China, also a symbol of our ancestors′ lofty ambition to unify the entire land. It was believed that he who got hold of the vessel for the midland would get the rest eight and would reign over the whole country. From this ancient saying one could easily see the vital importance of the region. Several millenniums have past. The central region are still full of vigor and vitality. In the south of the region, one will behold the magnificent Yellow Crane Tower looking over the Yangtze River, the grand reservoir contained in the Three Gorges, the mysterious jungles in Shenlongjia Natural Reserves, and the exotic peaks on Wudang Mountain; In the middle of the central region situate the historical Shaolin Temple renowned for its amazing Shaolin Kungfu, the Mausoleum of the Yellow Emperor, and the Qingmingshanghe Park in Kaifeng - the old capital city of Song Dynasty. In the west lie the vast Qingchuan plain that extends hundreds of miles, the tomb of Emperor Qinshihuang with the majestic terra-cotta warrior troops, the antique town of Pingyao, the Hukou Falls on the Yellow River and the towering Huashan Mountain with its precipitous peaks. Turning to the north, one will witness the imposing posture of the ″First Fortress under Heaven″, the Shanhaiguan Pass, the Mountain Resort and the Outlying Temples in Chengde, the labyrinthine reed marshes in Baiyangdian, as well as the heritage trails in the ancient cities like Xi'an and Taiyuan. But all in all, there is Beijing - the Capital of China. That is where the strongest heartbeat of the nation is heard.

With all these to our eyes and minds, how can we help but acclaim: What a wonderful wonderful land!

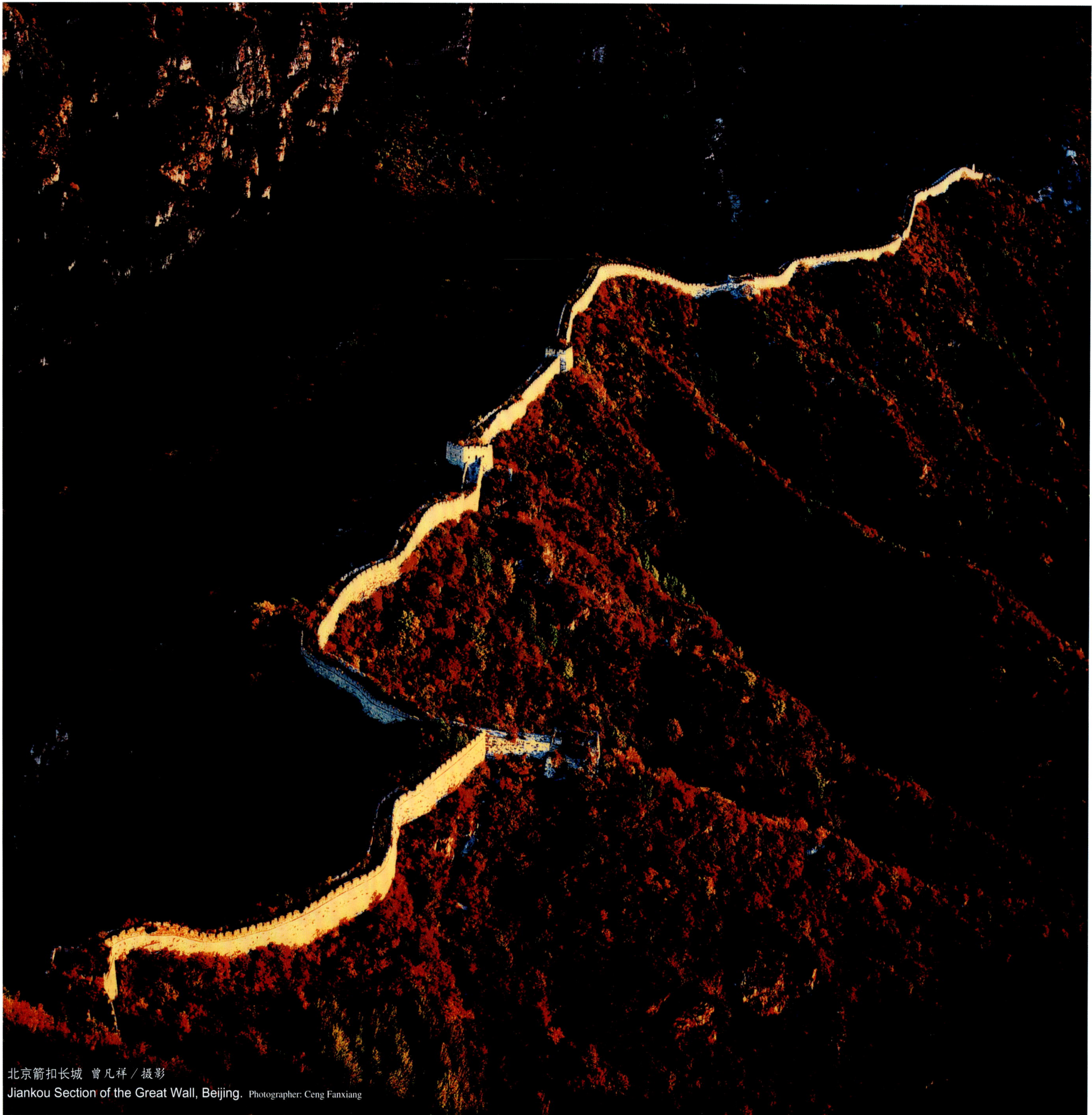

北京箭扣长城 曾凡祥／摄影
Jiankou Section of the Great Wall, Beijing. Photographer: Ceng Fanxiang

北京箭扣长城 张德文／摄影
Jiankou Section of the Great Wall, Beijing. Photographer: Zhang Dewen

北京箭扣长城 李同喜／摄影
Jiankou Section of the Great Wall, Beijing. Photographer: Li Tongxi

北京慕田峪长城 穆祥滨／摄影
The Great Wall at Mutianyu, Beijing. Photographer: Mu Xiangbin

北京石峡长城 李同喜／摄影
Shixia Section of the Great Wall, Beijing. Photographer: Li Tongxi

北京箭扣长城 刘双发／摄影
Jiankou Section of the Great Wall, Beijing. Photographer: Liu Shuangfa

北京猿人头骨复原 卞志武／摄影
A reconstructed bust of Peking Ape-man, Beijing.
Photographer: Bian Zhiwu

北京周口店猿人洞 卞志武／摄影
Cave of Peking Ape-man, Zhoukoudian, Beijing. Photographer: Bian Zhiwu

北京潭柘寺　卞志武／摄影
Tanzhe Temple, Beijing. Photographer: Bian Zhiwu

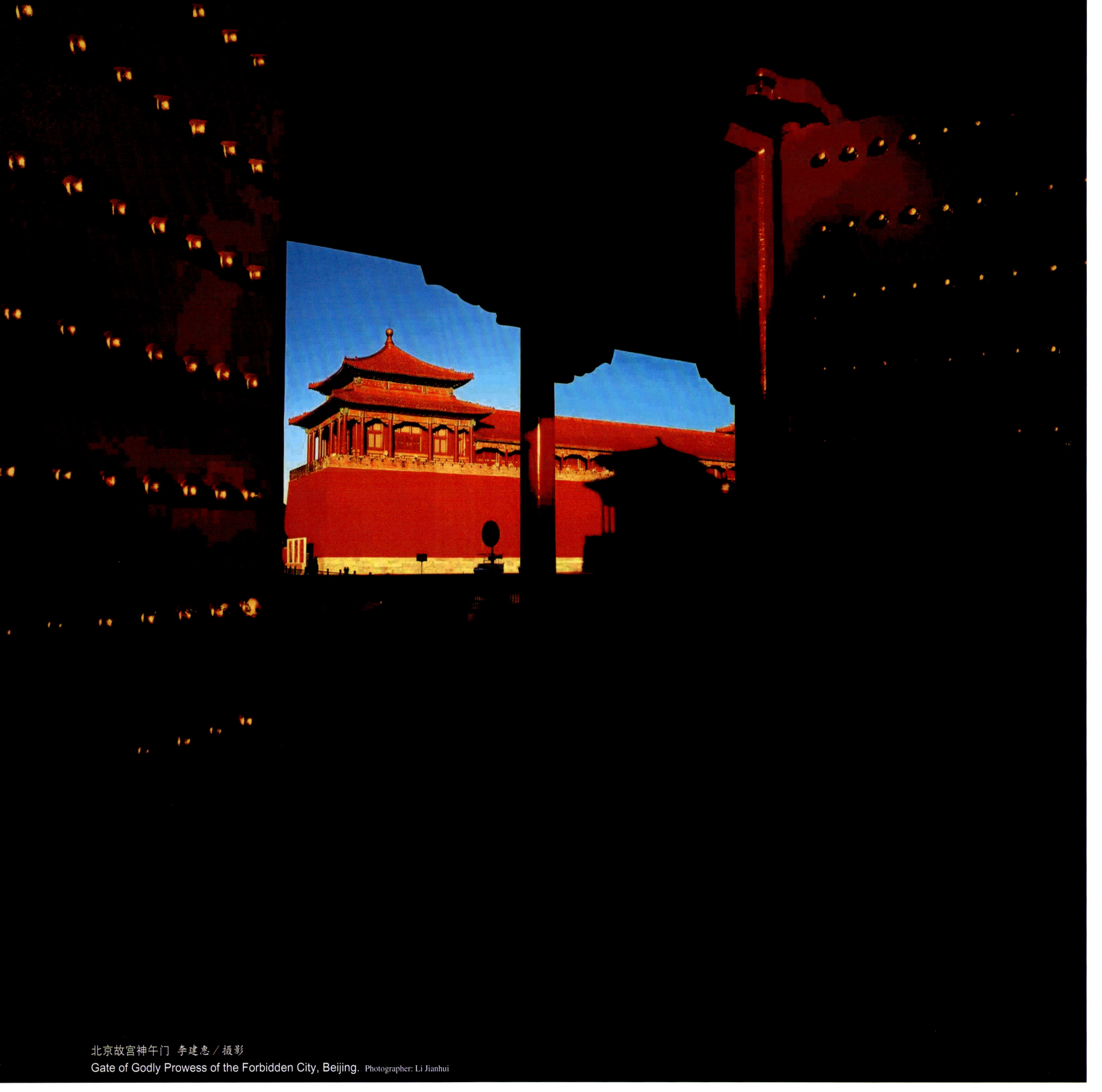

北京故宫神午门 李建惠／摄影
Gate of Godly Prowess of the Forbidden City, Beijing. Photographer: Li Jianhui

北京天坛祈年殿 郑启东／摄影
Hall of Prayer for Good Harvests, Temple of Heaven, Beijing. Photographer: Zheng Qidong

北京天坛祈年殿藻井 李 江／摄影
Ceiling of the Hall of Prayer for Good Harvests,Temple of Heaven, Beijing. Photographer: Li Jiang

中华人民共和国万岁

节日的北京天安门广场 卞志武／摄影
Tian'anmen Square on holiday, Beijing. Photographer: Bian Zhiwu

北京王府井　燕雨生／摄影
Wangfujing, Beijing. Photographer: Yan Yusheng

北京玉渊潭风光 郑启东／摄影
Jade Abyss Pool Park, Beijing. Photographer: Zheng Qidong

北京正阳门城楼夜色 郑启东／摄影
Night view of Zhengyangmen Gate, Beijing. Photographer: Zheng Qidong

北京四合院垂花门 卞志武／摄影
Gate in the Quadrangle compound, Beijing.
Photographer: Bian Zhiwu

北京昆明湖苏堤 孙玉芬／摄影
Su Causeway on the Kunming Lake, Beijing. Photographer: Sun Yufen

北京颐和园雪景 刘运光／摄影
Snow scene at the Summer Palace, Beijing. Photographer: Liu Yungua

北京颐和园十七孔桥 徐 明／摄影
The Seventeen Arch Bridge in the Summer Palace, Beijing. Photographer: Xu Ming

北京香山碧云寺金刚宝座塔 曾凡祥／摄影
Stupas in Biyun Temple on the Fragrant Hill, Beijing. Photographer: Zeng Fanxiang

北京中央商务区夜景 郑启东／摄影
Night view of the Central Business District of Beijing, Beijing. Photographer: Zheng Qidong

北京密云黑龙潭 彭小枫／摄影
Black Dragon Pool at Miyun County, Beijing. Photographer: Peng Xiaofeng

北京八达岭长城 郑启东／摄影
The Great Wall at Badaling, Beijing. Photographer: Zheng Qidong

北京圆明园遗址 杨佐桓／摄影
Ruins of Yuangmingyuan, Beijing. Photographer: Yang Zuohuan

天津天塔 Tianjin TV Tower

天津石家大院杨柳青（年画）博物馆
Museum of Yangliuqing New Year Pictures, Shi Family Courtyard, Tianjin.

天津劝业场 Tianjin Quanyechang Department Store.

天津盘山风景 Mt.Panshan,Tianjin.

天津港 Tianjin Port,Tianjin.

湖北神农架云海 杨铁军／摄影
Cloud Sea at Shennongjia Nature Reserve, Hubei Province. Photographer: Li Tiejun

湖北葛洲坝水利枢纽 李福堂／摄影
Geshouba Water Conservancy Project, Hubei Province. Photographer: Li Futang

湖北黄冈赤壁　李福堂／摄影

Chibi at Huanggang City, Hubei Province. Photographer: Li Futang

湖北襄樊古隆中　黄克勤／摄影
Gulongzhong scenic spot at Xiangfan City, Hubei Province. Photographer: Huang Keqin

湖北荆州古城 徐劲民／摄影
Ancient City of Jingzhou, Hubei Province. Photographer: Xu Jinmin

湖北武汉长江大桥和黄鹤楼　徐劲民／摄影
Wuhan Yangtze River Bridge and the Yellow Crane Pavilion, Hubei Province. Photographer: Xu Jinmin

湖北武汉三镇 熊克勇／摄影
Three Towns of Wuhan, Hubei Province. Photographer: Xiong Keyong

湖北荆州龙舟节 徐劲民／摄影
Dragon Boat Festival at Jinzhou, Hubei Province. Photographer: Xu Jinmin

湖北武汉磨山景区 童汉芳／摄影
Moshan Scenic Spot, Hubei Province. Photographer: Tong Hanfang

武汉东湖磨山梅园风光 张炳发／摄影
Moshan Plum Garden of Wuhan's East Lake, Hubei Province.
Photographer: Zheng Bingfa

湖北长阳武落钟离山 黄克勤／摄影

Mt. Wuluo Zhongli at Changyang Prefecture, Hubei Province. Photographer: Huang Keqin

长江三峡水利枢纽工程 廖德真／摄影

Three Gorges Project on the Yangtze River. Photographer: Liao Dezhen

左：河南洛阳出土的抬腿马与驯马俑
Left: Pottery horse and jockey excavated at Luoyang City, Henan Province.
右：河南洛阳二里头遗址出土的夏代乳钉纹铜爵
Right: Bronze wine container of Xia Dynasty excavated at Erligou village, Luoyang City, Henan Province.

河南洛阳龙门西山 李祥民／摄影
West Mountain at Longmen, Luoyang City,Henan Province. Photographer: Li Xiangmin

河南洛阳龙门卢舍那大佛 李祥民／摄影
Rocana Buddha at Longmen, Luoyang City, Henan Province. Photographer: Li Xiangmin

河南洛阳白马寺
White Horse Temple, Luoyang, Henan Province.

河南开封古吹台 贾吉祥／拍摄

Guchuitai, Kaifeng City, Henan Province. Photographer: Jia Jixiang

河南开封繁塔 贾吉祥／摄影
Fan Stupa, Kaifeng, Henan Province.
Photographer: Jia Jixiang

河南开封宋都御街夜色　贾吉祥／摄影

Night view of Song Dynasty Imperial Street in Kaifeng, Henan Province. Photographer: Jia Jixiang

河南焦作红石峡 彭小枫／摄影
Red Rock Valley, Jiaozuo, Henan Province. Photographer: Peng Xiaofeng

河南郑州黄河景区 赵绍钢／摄影
Scenic spot on Yellow River, Zhengzhou, Henan Province. Photographer: Zhao Shaogang

河南开封少林寺 宋慧娟／摄影
Shaolin Temple, Kaifeng, Henan Province. Photographer: Song Huijuan

河南嵩山 刘鲁豫／摄影
Mt. Songshan, Henan Province. Photographer:Liu Luyu

河北秦皇岛港 郭万海／摄影
The Port of Qinghuangdao, Hebei Province. Photographer: Guo Wanhai

河北北戴河之晨 郭万海／摄影
Beidaihe at dawn, Hebei Province. Photographer: Guo Wanhai

河北承德雾灵山风光 徐海斌／摄影
Mt. Wulingshan, Chengde, Hebei Province. Photographer: Xu Haibin

河北清西陵 张茂松／摄影
West Tombs of Qing Dynasty, Hebei Province. Photographer: Zhang Maosong

河北涞源白石山风光 徐海斌／摄影
White Stone Mountain at Laiyuan, Hebei Province. Photographer: Xu Haibin

河北太行山霞光　李自岐／摄影

Sunray upon Mt. Taihangshan, Hebei Province. Photographer: Li Ziqi

中法合资德尚葡萄酒庄园，座落在中国最佳的葡萄产区怀涿盆地，距八达岭长城仅10公里。庄园南借古燕山之阴，北取官厅湖之阳，占地达500公顷。
China-French joint venture-Chateau Des Champs, with an area of 500 hectares, is located by Guanting Lake and at the foot of Yan Mountain, 10krm to Badaling Great Wall.

河北白洋淀 卞志武／摄影
Baiyangdian Lake, Hebei Province. Photographer: Bian Zhiwu

河北坝上风光 陆其杰/摄影
Scenery of Bashang grassland, Hebei Province. Photographer: Lu Qijie

河北坝上白桦林 郑启东／摄影
Birch woods at Bashang, Hebei Province. Photographer: Zheng Qidong

河北坝上风光 刘　捷／摄影
Scenery of Bashang grassland, Hebei Province. Photographer: Liu Jie

河北坝上风光 金　宁／摄影
Scenery of Bashang grassland, Hebei Province. Photographer: Jin Ning

河北司马台长城 周万萍／摄影
The Great Wall at Simatai, Hebei Province. Photographer: Zhou Wanping

河北承德潘家口水下长城 李同喜／摄影
Under-water Great Wall at Panjiakou, Chengde,Hebei Province. Photographer: Li Tongxi

河北迁安喜峰口长城 李同喜／摄影
The Great Wall at Xifengkou, Qian'an,Hebei Province. Photographer: Li Tongxi

彩虹映照下的长城 周万萍／摄影
The Great Wall under the rainbow. Photographer: Zhou Wanping

雷电下的长城 周万萍／摄影
Lightening over the Great Wall. Photographer: Zhou Wanping

河北衡水湖 陆其杰／摄影
Hengshui Lake, Hebei Province. Photographer: Lu Qijie

陕西华山风光 孙晋强／摄影
Mt. Huashan, Shannxi Province. Photographer: Sun Jinqiang

陕西西安兵马俑　杨　茵／摄影
Terra-cotta soldiers and horses, Xi'an, Shannxi Province. Photographer: Yang Yin

陕西西安骊山 焦景泉／摄影
Mt. Lishan at Xi'an, Shannxi Province. Photographer: Jiao Jingquan

陕西西安大雁塔 秦 岭／摄影
Greater Wild Goose Pagoda, Xi'an, Shannxi Province. Photographer: Qinling

陕西西安小雁塔 焦景泉／摄影
Lesser Wild Goose Pagoda, Xi'an, Shannxi Province. Photographer: Jiao Jingquan

陕西扶风法门寺 薛天祥／摄影
Famen Temple in Fufeng county, Shannxi Province. Photographer: Xue Tianxiang

陕西宝鸡金台观 李胜利／摄影
Jintai Daoist Temple, Baoji, Shannxi Province. Photographer: Li Shengli

陕西宝鸡炎帝陵 秦 岭／摄影
Mausoleum of Emperor Yan at Baoji, Shannxi Province. Photographer: Qin Ling

陕西黄帝陵　卞志武／摄影
Mausoleum of Emperor Huang, Shannxi Province. Photographer: Bian Zhiwu

陕北安塞风情 冯立祥／摄影
Folk dance in Ansai County, Shannxi Province. Photographer: Feng Lixiang

陕西延安之晨 陈德通／摄影
Yan’an at dawn, Shannxi Province. Photographer: Chen Detong

山西恒山 郑启东／摄影

Mt. Hengshan, Shanxi Province. Photographer: Zheng Qidong

山西浑源悬空寺 郑启东／摄影 Hanging Temple, Hunyuan, Shanxi Province. Photographer: Zheng Qidong

山西应县木塔
Wooden Pagoda of Ying County, Shanxi Province.

山西五台山 Mt. Wutaishan, Shanxi Province.

山西大同云冈石窟 郑启东／摄影
Yungang Grottoes, Datong, Shanxi Province, Shanxi Province. Photographer: Zheng Qidong

山西太谷曹家大院 郑启东／摄影
Cao Family Mansion, Shanxi Province. Photographer: Zheng Qidong

山西祁县乔家大院 郑启东／摄影
Qiao Family Mansion, Shanxi Province. Photographer: Zheng Qidong

山西榆次常家庄园 郑启东／摄影
Chang Family Manor at Yuci, Shanxi Province. Photographer: Zheng Qidong

山西平遥古城
Pingyao Ancient City, Shanxi Province.

山西万家寨水库 王志文／摄影
Wanjiazhai Reservoir, Shanxi Province. Photographer: Wang Zhiwen

山西黄土高原　王志文／摄影

Loess Plateau, Shanxi Province. Photographer: Wang Zhiwen

山西黄河壶口瀑布 王 悦／摄影
Hukou Waterfall of the Yellow River, Shanxi Province. Photographer: Wang Yue

后　记

《江山如此多娇》大型摄影画册历时两年现予付梓。我们掩卷沉思，竟颇多感慨。

感慨之一，是国学大师启功先生于不久前仙逝，他生前“学为人师，行为世范”有口皆碑。本书得到他亲笔题写书名，不想如今已成绝笔之作。

感慨之二，是我们得到了全国各省、市、自治区，以及香港、澳门特别行政区政府相关部门的大力支持。特别要说的是，当我们征稿遇到困难时，众多摄影工作者伸出援手，不计名利，拿出了上乘佳作，使本书增色不少。

泱泱中华，江山多娇，艺海撷珍，挂一漏万。不足之处希望得到读者的教正，精彩之处愿为读者带来赏心悦目和快乐，是为后记。

另需说明的是，未标作者的作品系由相关省、市、自治区、特别行政区相关部门提供。在此，我们向作者表示感谢。

编　者

AFTERWORDS

After two years of hard work, the long expected photo album *A Land of Charm and Grandeur* has finally come to the press. As we sit back in reflection upon the out-coming of the book, we are beset with welling emotions.

One thing is about the great master Qi Gong who passed away quite recently. Being an accomplished scholar of the Chinese culture, Mr. Qi was universally acclaimed as a paragon of virtue and learning. Who would have thought that the inscription he wrote for the title of the album would become one of the last pieces of his autograph.

Another thing is about the generous support we have received from relevant government departments in all provinces, municipalities and autonomous regions, as well as from the SAR authorities in Hong Kong and Macao, to whom we owe our most sincere thanks. We are especially thankful to all those photographers who helped us out the predicaments by contributing the best of their works that have added great luster to the album.

The vast expanse of our motherland boasts so much charm and beauty that can never be compressed into one single album. What we have collected here are but a few drops from the ocean of art. It is our sincere hope that our readers will find the collection a delight to both their eyes and minds. We are also looking forward to comments and corrections.

P.S. Unnamed pictures are contributed by relevant departments of local governments. We thanks them as well.

Compiler

图书在版编目（CIP）数据

江山如此多娇／《江山如此多娇》编辑委员会编.
北京：当代世界出版社，2005.10
ISBN 7-80115-721-4/K · 129

Ⅰ.江…　Ⅱ.江…　Ⅲ.中国—概况—摄影集　Ⅳ.K92-64

中国版本图书馆 CIP 数据核字（2005）第 105130 号

书　　名　江山如此多娇
出版发行　当代世界出版社
地　　址　北京市复兴路 4 号（100860）
网　　址　http: //www.worldpress.com.cn
电　　话　（010）83908408　83908409　83908410（传真）
出　　品　北京东方光泽文化传播中心
经　　销　全国新华书店
责任编辑　张　勇
版式设计　王　欣
印　　刷　北京华联印刷有限公司
规　　格　787 × 1092　1/12
印　　张　34
版　　次　2005 年 10 月第 1 版
印　　次　2005 年 10 月第 1 次
印　　数　1—5000
定　　价　980.00 元